Food Dudes

THE MARS FAMILY:

M&M Mars Candy Makers

Joanne Mattern
ABDO Publishing Company

visit us at
www.abdopublishing.com

Published by ABDO Publishing Company, 8000 West 78th Street, Edina, Minnesota 55439.
Copyright © 2011 by Abdo Consulting Group, Inc. International copyrights reserved in all
countries. No part of this book may be reproduced in any form without written permission from the
publisher. The Checkerboard Library™ is a trademark and logo of ABDO Publishing Company.

Printed in the United States of America, North Mankato, Minnesota.
092010
012011

 PRINTED ON RECYCLED PAPER

Cover Photos: Alamy; Manuscripts and Archives, Yale University Library
Interior Photos: Alamy pp. 4, 9; AP Images pp. 18, 19, 21, 24; Galt Museum and Archives,
    Lethbridge, Alberta p. 8; Getty Images pp. 5, 14, 20, 25, 27; Granger Collection p. 17;
    iStockphoto pp. 7, 10; Manuscripts and Archives, Yale University Library pp. 1, 23;
    Minnesota Historical Society p. 11; O.C. Hognander p. 15; Photolibrary pp. 12–13, 16;
    Rick McNees p. 12; Washington Life Magazine p. 22

Series Coordinator: BreAnn Rumsch
Editors: Megan M. Gunderson, BreAnn Rumsch
Art Direction & Cover Design: Neil Klinepier

Library of Congress Cataloging-in-Publication Data

Mattern, Joanne, 1963-
  The Mars family : M&M Mars candy makers / Joanne Mattern.
    p. cm. -- (Food dudes)
  ISBN 978-1-61613-560-7
  1. Mars, Forrest--Juvenile literature. 2. Mars, Frank C., 1882-1934--Juvenile literature. 3. Mars,
Incorporated--History--Juvenile literature. 4. Businessmen--United States--Biography--Juvenile
literature. 5. Candy industry--United States--History--Juvenile literature. 6. Chocolate industry--
United States--History--Juvenile literature. I. Title.
  HD9330.C654M376 2011
  338.7'664153092273--dc22
  [B]
                        2010027940

Contents

Candy King

Mars Inc. is one of the biggest food manufacturers in the world. It is best known for making popular candies such as M&M's, Snickers, Milky Way, and 3 Musketeers. This family company's history began more than 125 years ago with the birth of Frank Mars.

The M was first printed on M&M's candies in 1950.

Franklin C. Mars was born on September 24, 1882. Frank began his life in Hancock, Minnesota, but he grew up in Saint Paul. There, his father worked as a **gristmill** operator. Mr. Mars did not make a lot of money, but he did bring home plenty of flour! Frank's mother, Alva, loved to bake. She used all that flour to make bread, cookies, pies, and cakes.

M&M's taste delicious alone or in baked treats!

At a young age, Frank caught **polio**. Although he recovered, he was never again able to stand or walk without a cane. So instead of playing outside, Frank stayed indoors with his mother.

To keep Frank busy in the house, Alva taught him to make candy. Frank grew up making caramels, fudge, and many other sweet treats.

By the time he was in high school, Frank was creating his own candy recipes. In 1901, he graduated from Breck School in Wilder, Minnesota. Frank was then ready to focus on his career.

Trial and Error

After graduation, Frank stuck with what he knew best, candy. By 1902, he was in charge of a candy company near Minneapolis, Minnesota. He sold Taylor's Molasses Chips to stores around the Minneapolis-Saint Paul area.

Soon, Frank met a schoolteacher named Ethel G. Kissack. In December 1902, they married. Then on March 21, 1904, they welcomed a son. Forrest Edward was born in Wadena, Minnesota.

Frank traveled a lot to try to sell more candy. He was often gone for weeks at a time. It took so long to get from store to store that Frank's candies often spoiled before he could sell them. As a result, the company soon went out of business.

Scared by their troubles, Ethel divorced Frank in 1910. Sadly, she soon found she could not care for Forrest on her own. So, she sent him to Canada to live with her parents.

Meanwhile, Frank remarried. His second wife was also named Ethel. They had a daughter named Patricia. Then, Frank and his new family moved to Washington State. There, he continued working

Thanks to the Mississippi River, Minneapolis became an industrial center in the late 1800s.

to find success in the candy business. After several failed attempts, Frank returned to Minnesota in 1920.

In Minneapolis, Frank started the Mar-O-Bar Company. It was named after a candy he had invented. Frank's customers enjoyed his Mar-O-Bars, but they liked his butter cream candies even better. Frank sold a lot of butter creams! By 1923, he finally had a successful business.

Growing Up

Meanwhile, Forrest spent his childhood with his grandparents. They lived in North Brattleford, Saskatchewan, in Canada. Forrest's

Lethbridge Central School

mother wrote to him often. However, he did not see his father at all while he was growing up.

Forrest grew to be a smart boy who liked school. He walked about three miles (5 km) to get there each day! Forrest's best subject was mathematics. He also had many interests outside of school. Forrest liked to read and learn **trivia**. He also liked to play games such as chess, cribbage, and poker.

In 1922, Forrest graduated from Lethbridge Central School in Alberta, Canada. He received a **scholarship** to attend the University of California at Berkeley. There, Forrest studied mining.

During college, Forrest worked in the university's kitchen. He also discovered how to be a businessman. He bought meat and sold it to the kitchen's chefs. It didn't take long before Forrest was making about $100 each week! He then stopped studying to focus on his business interests.

From science to art, Berkeley is one of today's top U.S. universities.

Father and Son

In summer 1923, Forrest found work as a traveling salesman. During a trip to Chicago, Illinois, he posted advertisements on all the major buildings along State Street. Forrest was arrested for this, and the newspapers wrote about it.

Frank heard about what had happened to his son. He went to the jail to post Forrest's **bail**. It was the first time Forrest had seen his father since he was six years old. After Forrest was released, he and Frank went to a **soda fountain** together.

When Milky Way bars were first sold, their large size impressed customers!

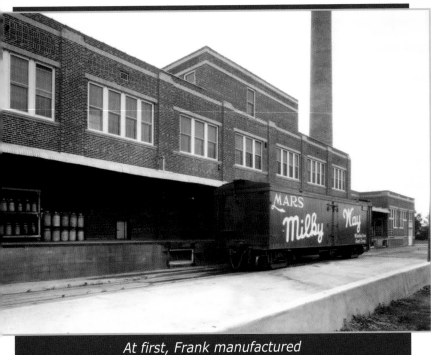

At first, Frank manufactured Milky Way bars in Minnesota.

The two men did not want to talk about the past. Instead, they talked about business. Forrest suggested that Frank make a candy bar that tasted like the chocolate malts they were drinking. Frank thought this was a great idea. When he returned to Minnesota, he invented a new candy bar.

Frank's Milky Way bar was made of malt-flavored **nougat**. On top of this filling, Frank added a layer of caramel. He covered the whole thing with a solid chocolate coating. In 1924, Frank started selling Milky Way bars for a nickel each. People loved the big, fluffy chocolate treat! By the end of the year, sales of Milky Way bars reached almost $800,000.

Making Money

The Mars home in River Forest near Chicago

After his time in Chicago, Forrest went back to California. Then in 1925, he transferred to the Sheffield Scientific School at Yale University in New Haven, Connecticut. There, he studied industrial engineering.

At the same time, Forrest read every book he could about successful companies. He was serious, driven, and had a natural understanding of business. Forrest told Frank he could save money by moving his business to Chicago. Frank listened to his son's advice. In 1927, he began construction on a new factory there.

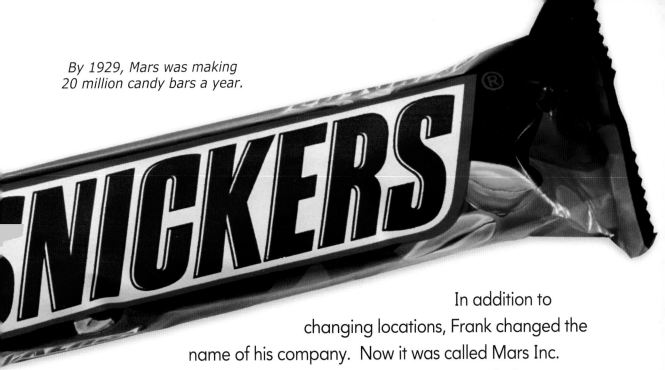

By 1929, Mars was making
20 million candy bars a year.

In addition to changing locations, Frank changed the name of his company. Now it was called Mars Inc. After Forrest graduated from Yale in 1928, he went to work there.

During the 1930s, Frank continued to invent candy bars. In 1930, he introduced the Snickers bar. It combined peanuts, **nougat**, caramel, and chocolate. In 1932, Frank came up with the 3 Musketeers bar. At first, this chocolate-covered bar had three pieces of nougat in vanilla, chocolate, and strawberry. When the price of strawberries went up, Frank switched to one large piece of chocolate nougat.

By 1932, Mars Inc. was selling more than $25 million of chocolate a year. The only U.S. candy company that was bigger was the Hershey Chocolate Company. Frank was happy with his success, but Forrest wanted more. "I wanted to conquer the whole world," he said.

Torn Apart

Milky Way Farm was home to Frank's racehorse Gallahadion.
He won the Kentucky Derby in 1940.

Early on in his career, Forrest met a young woman named Audrey Meyer. The two fell in love and married in 1930. Soon, they started a family. Their son Forrest Edward Jr. was born on August 13, 1931. John Franklin was born on October 1, 1935. Their daughter Jacqueline Anne arrived on October 10, 1939.

The Mars mausoleum in Lakewood Cemetery

Meanwhile, Frank was enjoying his wealth. In 1930, he started a horse farm in Tennessee called Milky Way Farm. There, he bred racehorses.

Although both men seemed happy, Frank and Forrest often argued. One day, Forrest asked Frank to give him part of the company. Frank said no. Instead, Frank gave Forrest the right to sell the Milky Way bar in Europe. So in 1932, Forrest moved to Paris, France, with his young family.

Then on April 8, 1934, Frank suddenly died of kidney failure and heart disease. He was just 50 years old. Frank was buried on his farm. Today, he rests in the Mars family **mausoleum** in a Minneapolis cemetery.

Life in Europe

Forrest Sr. did not return to the United States for Frank's funeral. He was busy building his business, Mars Ltd., in Europe. Forrest Sr. wanted to learn everything he could about making chocolate.

In 1933, Forrest Sr. had traveled to Switzerland. There, he had worked in the chocolate factories of Jean Tobler and Henri Nestlé. These famous **chocolatiers** thought Forrest was just a factory worker. They had no idea he was there to learn their secrets!

Later that year, Forrest Sr. started his own small factory in Slough, England. His young family

Forrest Sr. found success in England with Mars Ltd. By 1939, this branch was the third-largest candy maker in Great Britain.

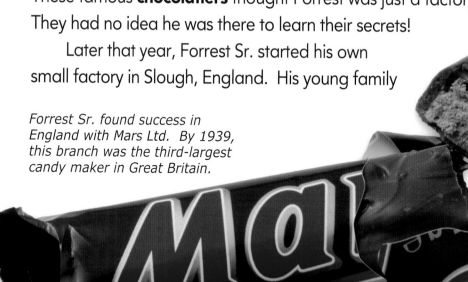

lived in a small apartment behind the factory. They faced trying times with little food and few comforts.

Forrest Sr. poured his energy into his work. He made a sweeter version of the Milky Way bar. Forrest Sr. called it the Mars bar. Soon, the Mars bar was very popular in England.

In 1934, Forrest Sr. bought a British pet food company. It was called Chappel Bros Ltd., or Chappie's. Chappie's was the beginning of the Mars company's pet food business. Within five years, Forrest Sr. had increased his pet food sales five times over.

Back in the United States, Mars bars debuted in 1936. These candy bars had almonds in them.

it's the Chocolate-
it's the Nougat-
it's the Nuts!

MARS...the 3-flavor candy bar

Honest-to-goodness MILK CHOCOLATE · Creamy NOUGAT · Toasted whole ALMONDS

M&M's Magic

Original M&M's packaging from 1940

While traveling in Europe, Forrest Sr. had visited Spain. There, he had seen soldiers eating small pieces of chocolate. A sugar coating kept the chocolate from melting. Forrest Sr. thought this was an amazing idea!

When **World War II** began in 1939, Forrest Sr. and his family returned to the United States. Forrest Sr. had not forgotten about the candy-coated chocolates he saw in Spain. He wanted to share his discovery with someone who could help him produce it.

That same year, he met with William Murrie in Hershey, Pennsylvania. Murrie was president of the Hershey Chocolate Company. At the meeting, Forrest Sr. took a handful of the candy-coated chocolates out of his pocket. He told Murrie the candies had been in his pocket all through his long train ride there. Murrie was impressed.

Forrest Sr. said that he wanted Murrie's son Bruce to be his partner in a new candy business. He wanted Hershey to supply the chocolate. Forrest Sr. also suggested they call the candy M&M's. One *M* would stand for Mars. The other *M* would stand for Murrie. William and Bruce Murrie agreed to this plan.

In 1940, M&M Ltd. opened for business in Newark, New Jersey. Soon they were supplying M&M's to U.S. troops. Soldiers loved M&M's because the candy did not melt.

After the war ended, people in the United States learned they loved M&M's too. In 1954, the famous M&M's **slogan** was introduced. It said the milk chocolate "melts in your mouth, not in your hands." By 1956, M&M's was the most popular candy in America.

M&M's have remained so popular that they are even stocked on Air Force One, the U.S. president's airplane.

More than Candy

Forrest Sr. liked selling candy, but most of all he liked starting new businesses. In 1941, he heard about a rice mill near Houston, Texas. Employees there had developed a new way to process rice. This way, it held more of its **nutrients**. The rice also cooked quickly and was very fluffy.

In 1942, Forrest Sr. bought the rice mill. Then he worked to find the best rice for the mill's process. Forrest Sr. finally chose a type of rice grown by a farmer named Ben. He named his new company after the farmer, calling it Uncle Ben's Inc. This brand went on to become an important part of the Mars company.

In 1965, Mars Electronics International was created in Great Britain. The company expanded to the United States in 1967. Mars Electronics introduced electronic vending machines.

Forrest Sr. also expanded his pet food business to the United States. In 1968, he bought a company called Kal Kan. In 1988, Kal Kan Dog Food was renamed Pedigree. Kal Kan Cat Food was renamed Whiskas. Both brands are still popular today.

The Pedigree dog food brand plays a large role in supporting pet adoption.

Family Ties

Candy, rice, electronics, and pet food companies were not enough for Forrest Sr. He still wanted to buy his father's part of the business. Frank's wife refused to sell to Forrest Sr. But after her death in 1945, Forrest Sr. inherited half of her **shares**. In December 1964, he purchased all the remaining shares of his father's company. This made him the sole owner of Mars Inc. Forrest Sr. then made all of his food businesses part of Mars Inc.

Jacqueline Mars

Growing up with the king of candy as your father may sound fun. However, Forrest Jr., John, and Jacqueline had an ordinary childhood. Though the family was wealthy, they did not have any hired household help.

Forrest Sr. did not want his children to be spoiled. So if the children wanted something, they had

Forrest Mars Jr.

John Mars

to work to earn the money. Their parents did not buy them fancy clothes or expensive cars. They did not receive allowances. They didn't even get free candy!

Forrest Jr. graduated from Yale in 1953. John also attended Yale before serving in the U.S. Army from 1956 to 1958. After their education, Forrest Sr. trained his children to work for him. If he didn't like their work, he made sure they knew it. Even though they were family, Forrest Sr. treated his children no differently than other employees.

Quiet Years

Mars began using machines to produce candies in 1953. Workers still make sure every candy is of good quality.

Forrest Sr. was demanding of his family as well as his employees. He wanted every product to be perfect. If it was not, he would throw it away and make his workers start the job over again. However, Mars workers earned a good income. They were also encouraged to share their ideas with Forrest Sr.

In 1969, Forrest Sr. retired from Mars Inc. Forrest Jr. and John took over the company. Jacqueline later became a leader at the company too.

After Forrest Sr. retired, he didn't stop working altogether. In 1980, he started a new candy company in Henderson, Nevada. He

named the company Ethel M Chocolates after his mother. In 2003, Ethel M Chocolates became part of Mars Inc.

Forrest Sr. lived quietly during his retirement. He was a very private man. In fact, he never talked about the company. Instead, he let his children take care of the business. Forrest Jr., John, and Jacqueline are very private too.

Forrest Sr. died in Miami, Florida, on July 1, 1999. He was 95 years old. When he died, Forrest was worth more than $4 billion. He was one of the richest men in the United States.

Mars Today

Mars continued to be a successful company under Forrest Sr.'s children. The company introduced several new products. They began selling Skittles candies in 1979. In 1986, they developed a popular granola and chocolate bar called Kudos. They also created a filled pretzel snack called Combos.

In 1986, Mars gained a company called Dove International. In 1991, Mars used the rich Dove chocolate to make its popular Dove Promises chocolates. Then in 1989, Mars began manufacturing ice cream versions of 3 Musketeers, Snickers, and Milky Way bars.

In 2008, the Mars company became even bigger when it bought the William Wrigley Jr. Company. Wrigley's had been making chewing gum and other candy products for more than 100 years. Adding this business to Mars created an even more successful company.

The Mars family sells its products in more than 180 countries. The company uses the latest machinery in their clean, well-managed factories. The Mars commitment to quality and excellence makes products that people and animals enjoy all over the world.

Mars makes 7 of the world's top 20 chocolate snacks.

Timeline

1882	Franklin C. Mars was born on September 24 in Hancock, Minnesota.
1904	On March 21, Forrest Edward Mars was born in Wadena, Minnesota.
1920	Frank started the Mar-O-Bar Company in Minneapolis, Minnesota.
1924	Frank started selling Milky Way bars for a nickel each.
1928	Forrest Sr. went to work at his father's company, now called Mars Inc.
1932	Forrest Sr. moved to Europe to sell the Milky Way bar.
1934	On April 8, Frank Mars died.
1940	Forrest Sr. started M&M Ltd. in Newark, New Jersey.
1964	Forrest Sr. became the sole owner of Mars Inc.
1969	Forrest Sr. retired; Forrest Jr. and John took over Mars Inc.
1999	On July 1, Forrest Mars Sr. died.
2008	Mars Inc. bought the William Wrigley Jr. Company.

Fun Bites

When M&M's were created, they quickly became the top candy in the United States. Today, M&M's rank as the world's most popular candy. Here are a few fun tidbits about this delicious snack:

A single M&M's candy piece is called a lentil. More than 400 million lentils are produced in the United States each day!

Today's M&M's varieties include milk chocolate, dark chocolate, peanut, peanut butter, almond, and pretzel.

Mars changes the mix of M&M's colors according to changes in consumer tastes. Occasionally, the company also lets consumers vote for a new color. In 1995, 10 million people voted to add the color blue.

In 1982, M&M's made history as the first candy eaten in space. M&M's have been sent on shuttle missions ever since.

Mars scientists specially formulated the flavor of the chocolate used in M&M's to taste refreshing rather than sweet. This is what keeps you coming back for more!

Glossary

bail - a deposit of money needed to temporarily release a prisoner. It guarantees that the prisoner will later attend trial.

chocolatier - a maker or seller of chocolate candy.

gristmill - a mill for grinding grain.

mausoleum - a large tomb that is usually stone and above ground.

nougat - a fluffy filling made with whipped egg whites and corn syrup.

nutrient - a substance found in food and used in the body. It promotes growth, maintenance, and repair.

polio - the common name for poliomyelitis. This disease usually affects children and sometimes leaves people paralyzed.

scholarship - a gift of money to help a student pay for instruction.

share - one of the equal parts into which the ownership of a company is divided.

slogan - a word or a phrase used to express a position, a stand, or a goal.

soda fountain - a store with a counter for preparing and serving sodas, sundaes, and ice cream.

trivia - facts of little or no importance.

World War II - from 1939 to 1945, fought in Europe, Asia, and Africa. Great Britain, France, the United States, the Soviet Union, and their allies were on one side. Germany, Italy, Japan, and their allies were on the other side.

Web Sites

To learn more about the Mars family, visit ABDO Publishing Company online. Web sites about the Mars family are featured on our Book Links page. These links are routinely monitored and updated to provide the most current information available.

www.abdopublishing.com

Index